The Gig Economy Redux

How Blockchain is Empowering Freelancers and Entrepreneurs

Table of Contents

Chapter 1. Introduction

Within the thriving realm of the gig economy, a groundbreaking shift is currently unveiling, anchored by blockchain technology. In our special report, "The Gig Economy Redux: How Blockchain is Empowering Freelancers and Entrepreneurs," we walk you through this compelling progression, elucidating how blockchain is empowering a new generation of freelancers and entrepreneurs. Guarantees of transparency, trust, and security define this new landscape, unlocking innovative opportunities for individual professionals and startups alike. By delicately marrying technical insight with down-to-earth explanation, this report will give you a comprehensive appreciation of the changes unfolding. This is not just about prime technological evolution; it's about the dawn of a new era in the gig economy, where freedom, control, and entrepreneurship take a stronger presence than they ever have before. We invite you to journey with us into this exciting frontier, and discover the prospects that are waiting for you to seize.

Chapter 2. The Gig Economy: A Defining Overview

The gig economy, often interchangeably called the sharing, freelance, or on-demand economy, refers to a labor market paradigm centred around short-term contracts or freelance work as opposed to permanent jobs. This model challenges traditional employment, instigating a shift from conventional, long-term contracts to a more fragmented, flexible, and autonomous mode of working.

2.1. The Evolution of the Gig Economy

From the post-war era to the end of the 20th century, the labor market was predominantly characterized by fixed employment relations. Employees were guaranteed stable wages and secure working conditions in return for their loyalty and long-term commitment. However, rapid advancements in technology have disrupted this status quo, facilitating the rise of the gig economy.

While the Internet revolution of the 1990s saw the seeds of the gig economy being planted with the advent of remote work and digital marketplaces, it was the proliferation of smartphones and mobile broadband that truly catalyzed its exponential growth. The ease of digital connectivity and the ubiquity of smart devices transformed convenience into a business model, leading to the emergence of on-demand service platforms such as Uber, Airbnb, and TaskRabbit.

The financial crisis of 2008 further boosted the gig economy's profile as a viable and attractive labor model. As conventional employment opportunities dwindled in the aftermath of the economic downturn, many workers turned to gig platforms for supplemental income streams. In tandem, businesses also adapted demands for greater operational flexibility.

2.2. Key Characteristics of the Gig Economy

There are several defining factors of the gig economy.

First, this economic model is typified by flexibility. Gig workers often enjoy the ability to choose when, where, and how they work. They have the freedom to balance work with other commitments, whether that's a personal passion, a side hustle, or family responsibilities.

Second, jobs in the gig economy tend to be project-based, with workers hired for specific tasks or short-term assignments instead of full-time positions.

Third, digital platforms play a significant role in the gig economy. They connect workers with potential employers or customers, serving as vehicles for advertising, bidding, scheduling, and sometimes, delivering the work.

Lastly, gig workers are generally treated as independent contractors rather than employees. This allows businesses to cut down on labor costs, but it also means gig workers often lack benefits and job security.

2.3. The Impact of the Gig Economy

While the gig economy offers several advantages, such as flexibility and autonomy, it also has its share of criticisms. The lack of job security, potential income instability, and the absence of benefits like health insurance or retirement savings plans can create precarious work conditions for some gig workers.

However, the gig economy has democratized access to work

opportunities. It has allowed spaces for marginalized groups, such as those with disabilities, or people living in rural communities, to find gainful employment. Moreover, it allows individuals to monetize their personal assets, skills, or time.

On a broader scale, the gig economy disrupts traditional business models. Companies can tap into a global talent pool, thereby enabling a more distributed and scalable workforce. Meanwhile, traditional businesses are being forced to redefine their practices to compete with efficient and adaptive gig platforms.

2.4. The Gig Economy and Blockchain

The rise of blockchain technology promises to further reshape the gig economy. Blockchain, as a distributed ledger technology, can provide an immutable record of transactions, bringing transparency and trust to gig platforms.

Smart contracts, a particular feature of blockchain, can revolutionize the gig economy, ensuring secure payments and enforcement of work agreements. It could potentially automate various managerial tasks like hiring, time-tracking, and payment processes, thus reducing costs and increasing efficiency. With blockchain, gig economy platforms could become more autonomous, disintermediated, and democratized.

In conclusion, the gig economy has grown rapidly over the past few decades and will continue to evolve. Technology has been a crucial driver of this change, and the emergence of blockchain technology presents exciting prospects for the future of work. As we continue to explore the convergence of these forces through this report, it's important to understand the complexities and transformative potential that lie at the intersection of the gig economy and blockchain technology.

Chapter 3. Unraveling the Blockchain: Key Principles

Before embarking on an exploration of the profound impact blockchain technology has on the gig economy, it's essential to have a solid understanding of the fundamental principles that underpin this groundbreaking technology. Blockchain, while relatively young, is undeniably robust and powerful, making it the ideal foundation for a more decentralized and transparent gig economy. This overview will delineate the basic concepts, elements, and mechanisms of blockchain technology.

3.1. Anatomy of a Blockchain

At its core, a blockchain is a continuously growing list of records, known as blocks, which are interconnected and secured using cryptographic principles. Each block contains a cryptographic hash of the previous block, a timestamp, and transaction data.

The unique design of a blockchain allows for the distribution of digital information but not its duplication. Thus, each individual piece of data can only have one owner at any given time, eliminating the issues of double-spending and fraud. It's this fundamental quality that makes it an engaging and revolutionary technology.

3.2. Decentralization and Distributed Ledger Technology

One key principle that sets blockchain technology apart from traditional data structures is decentralization. Unlike traditional databases that rely on a central authority or entity, blockchain runs on a network of computers, also known as nodes. Each node in the network maintains a copy of the entire blockchain, thereby creating a distributed ledger, a record of all transactions accessible to all nodes in the network.

This essentially means that no single entity has complete control over the entirety of the data. Instead, control is distributed across the network, making blockchains inherently resistant to data manipulation or single points of failure. This approach fosters transparency and trust among participants - both vital tenets in a thriving gig economy.

3.3. Cryptography and Security

Blockchain owes much of its reputability to the security derived from cryptographic principles. Transactions on the blockchain are secured through a process known as hashing, which transforms input data of any size into a fixed, unique string of characters. This output, called a hash, undergoes verification by the network's nodes.

To protect from alteration, each block's hash includes the hash of the previous block, effectively "chaining" the blocks together. Any changes to a block's data would necessitate a new hash, collapsing the chain's continuity. Hence, blockchains are practically immutable, enhancing their suitability to hold contractual obligations in the gig economy.

3.4. Mining and Consensus Protocols

Blockchain networks uphold their integrity through consensus protocols, rules that dictate how participating nodes agree on the validity of transactions. One widely adopted consensus protocol is Proof-of-Work (PoW), used by Bitcoin and other prominent blockchains.

In PoW, nodes, referred to as miners, compete to add new transaction records to the blockchain. The 'work' involves solving a complex mathematical puzzle, and thus requires substantial computational resources. Upon successful puzzle completion, the miner presents their solution to the network. If a majority of the nodes agree (hence the term consensus), the transactions are validated and added to the blockchain as a new block. This process, while resource-intensive, safeguards against fraudulent or conflicting transactions.

3.5. Smart Contracts

A final key principle to understanding blockchain is the concept of smart contracts. Essentially, a smart contract is a self-enforcing agreement embedded in computer code. It is triggered and executed automatically upon the fulfilment of predefined conditions.

In the context of the gig economy, a freelancer and a client could enter into a smart contract for a project. The contract could stipulate that funds will be released to the freelancer after they deliver the project within a specified timeframe. Smart contracts, therefore, foster confidence and security in peer-to-peer transactions, an essential characteristic nourishing the gig economy.

Through this comprehensive overview of blockchain's defining principles, it becomes evident why the technology has emerged as a pivotal influencer of the gig economy. It fosters decentralization, ensures high-level security through cryptography, enforces integrity through mining and consensus protocols, and enables the applications of smart contracts.

These fundamentals form the bedrock of blockchain technology. Understanding them serves as the starting point of recognizing the force that is transforming the modus operandi of the gig economy. The impact of these blockchain mechanisms on various facets of the gig economy will be the subject of our forthcoming chapters. Let's continue the journey.

Chapter 4. Blockchain and its Impact on the Freelancer's Trust Environment

In today's ever-evolving world, the trust environment of freelancers is being fundamentally reshaped by blockchain technology. The quintessential combination of transparency, security, and decentralization that blockchain offers has enabled freelancers to engage with their clients in a more efficient and transparent manner, significantly enhancing their trust environment.

4.1. Understanding Trust in Freelancing Environment

The concept of trust plays a critical role in the freelancing ecosystem. Given the remote and often international nature of freelancing projects, the risk concerns are inevitable. Freelancers often face challenges such as payment defaults, contract breaches, and inefficient dispute resolution. On the other hand, clients may harbor doubts about the freelancer's reliability, professionalism, and quality of work. This is where blockchain technology, with its inherent characteristics, comes to play.

4.2. How Does Blockchain Enhance Trust?

Blockchain technology can build a comprehensive trust environment for freelancers through decentralization, transparency, and security. Its decentralized nature fundamentally alters the way trust is conceived and maintained.

- Decentralization: Typically, trust is established through intermediary institutions like banks, online platforms, or third-party arbitration services. However, these entities can be biased, inefficient, and sometimes, even corrupt. Blockchain removes the need for these middlemen by providing a decentralized network where transactions are verified by a network of computers. Thus, the trust is built on the robustness of the technology itself rather than relying on human entities.

- Transparency: All transactions on the blockchain are visible to every participant in the network, eliminating the possibility of fraudulent practices. This transparency allows freelancers to prove their credibility and reputation through a verifiable record of their past transactions and thereby secure future contracts more confidently.

- Security: Blockchain relies on advanced cryptographic techniques to ensure the security and integrity of data. Once a transaction is recorded on the blockchain, it is almost impossible to alter or delete it. This offers freelancers a strong assurance that their work and payments will be secured and cannot be tampered with.

4.3. Blockchain-Enabled Freelancing Platforms

New platforms leveraging the power of blockchain technology are emerging and changing the freelancing landscape. These platforms work on the principle of smart contracts, which are self-executing contracts with the terms of agreement directly written into code.

For example, a freelancer might sign a smart contract with a client that specifies that once the agreed-upon work is submitted and approved by the client, the payment will automatically be transferred to the freelancer's account. This eliminates the need for a middleman and ensures that the freelancer gets paid on time.

4.4. A Case Study: Blockchain in Graphic Design Freelancing

Consider a graphic design freelancer who is working with numerous international clients. Prior to the advent of blockchain, they had to rely heavily on trust and the credibility of intermediaries. Now, they can use a blockchain-based freelance platform.

On these platforms, the freelancer's work, revisions, and client feedback are all recorded on the blockchain, providing a transparent evidence of their professional history. When a new client considers hiring this freelancer, they can see a trustable trace of their previous accomplishments, enhancing the prospect for both parties to engage in trustworthy business relationship.

Furthermore, the payment process is automated via smart contracts, ensuring that the freelancer gets paid as soon as the work is approved. This eliminates the uncertainty and stress from the payment process, allowing the freelancer to focus entirely on their work.

4.5. Conclusive Remarks: The Future of Trust in Freelancing

Blockchain technology's impact on the trust environment in freelancing is significant. The security, transparency, and decentralization provided by blockchain fundamentally reframes how trust is built and maintained in this field. It empowers freelancers and clients to engage in transparent, secure, and efficient contractual relationships.

Despite the challenges in implementation and adoption that blockchain faces today, its potential benefits for freelancers and the gig economy as a whole are enormous. As more freelancing platforms embrace blockchain and as more freelancers recognize its advantages, it's clear that blockchain will play a crucial role in shaping the future of trust in the freelancing ecosystem. Its powerful benefits indeed pave the way for a more reliable, robust, and revolutionised gig economy.

Chapter 5. Economic Autonomy: How Blockchain Facilitates Entrepreneurial Spirit

In order to understand how blockchain technology is revolutionizing freelancing and entrepreneurship, it is important to first take a step back and set the stage. Blockchain, a distributed, peer-to-peer (P2P) technology, was first introduced by an anonymous person (or group) named Satoshi Nakamoto in 2008. The technology served as the underpinning for Bitcoin, the world's first cryptocurrency. Since then, blockchain has undergone significant evolution and expansion, shining in its multifunctional functionality and presenting profound implications for numerous sectors. Its potential in the realm of the gig economy stands out as one of the most promising areas of application.

5.1. The Trustless, Peer-to-Peer Economy

Blockchain's most well-known trait is its decentralized nature. This means transactions are not controlled and facilitated by a central authority, such as a financial institution, but are managed autonomously across a network of nodes. The transactional data is stored on blocks that are transparently linked into a chain. Each of these blocks is publicly auditable and cryptographically secure, resulting in a system that is inherently resistant to fraud, manipulation, and single points of failure. This 'trustless' economy, where the need for middlemen is obsolete, has substantial benefits for freelancers and entrepreneurs worldwide.

By creating direct pathways between service providers and clients, freelancers can now bypass the exuberant fees and restrictions of intermediary platforms. Clients, on the other hand, enjoy the assurance of transparent processes and the reliability of blockchain-secured deliverables. In essence, the playing field becomes more equitable, with opportunities democratically accessible to anyone, anywhere, regardless of local financial infrastructure or geopolitical barriers.

5.2. Tokenization of Skills and Time

One of the most transformative aspects of blockchain technology in the gig economy is the tokenization of skills and time. This means breaking down professional services into granular, tradable assets represented by tokens. A designer, for example, can tokenize an hour of design work, making it something tangible to be traded, sold or bought on the blockchain.

This literal 'token' of value can then be easily and securely transferred between parties, allowing for more flexible and efficient ways of working. Freelancers can price their services in a way that best represents their value, and clients can precisely purchase what they need. This opens up radical possibilities for commodity markets oriented around professional services.

5.3. Instant, Cross-Border Payments

The combination of blockchain and cryptocurrency also resolves one of the major pain points of the global gig economy: delayed payments and high transaction fees. Instead of being reliant on banks and traditional financial services, payments are handled over the blockchain.

This not only means that transactions can be processed instantaneously, regardless of geographical location, but that transaction fees are minimized. This is especially beneficial for freelancers and entrepreneurs working with international clients, as it allows for seamless and cost-effective cross-border financial transfers. Adding to this, the ability to transact in cryptocurrency has the added advantage of being immunized against inflation and currency devaluation in unstable economies.

5.4. Smart Contracts and Automated Agreements

Incorporating 'Smart Contracts' is one of the ways that blockchain technology breathes new life into the gig economy. These self-executing contracts carry the terms of an agreement in code, and the contract automatically triggers payment or the next phase of the process when certain predefined conditions are met.

For freelancers, this means a guarantee of payment upon delivery without the need for a third-party escrow service – the contract itself ensures it. No longer must professionals wait for their clients to manually process transactions, often long after the work is done. For clients, this creates a more trustworthy and efficient environment, as payment only occurs when agreed-upon milestones are met or tasks completed successfully.

5.5. Empowering Entrepreneurial Spirit

Above all, blockchain technology amplifies the entrepreneurial spirit that fuels the gig economy. It transcends physical borders, shatters financial barriers, and empowers individuals to take control of their economic destiny. Entrepreneurs are no longer confined by the limits of their local economies. Instead, they are connected with a global marketplace where their skills and services can be transparently tokenized, traded, and transacted.

Blockchain-enabled freelance platforms provide the infrastructure for this new economy, tying together the peer-to-peer interaction, tokenization, instant cross-border payments, and Smart Contracts. In this system, entrepreneurs retain full control of their work, securely manage their agreements, and claim maximum value from their contributions.

In summary, blockchain doesn't just change the mechanics of the gig economy; it redefines the very principles upon which it operates. This ensures that the gig economy no longer remains a fallback, but emerges as a sought-after avenue, exemplifying professional autonomy, financial independence, and entrepreneurial freedom.

Indeed, the stage is set for a new era in the gig economy - one that leverages the power of blockchain technology to unlock unprecedented economic autonomy for millions of freelancers and entrepreneurs around the world. The possibilities are vast, the potential is enormous, and the time for transformation is now. As we shift towards this new paradigm, embracing change and adapting will no longer be optional but essential to thrive.

Chapter 6. Smart Contracts: Streamlining Transactions in the Gig Economy

In the heart of the intersection between blockchain technology and the gig economy, smart contracts stand as instrumental game-changers. These self-executing contracts, with the terms of the agreement recorded onto a distributed, decentralized blockchain network, present a robust solution to many challenges inherent to traditional financial transactions.

6.1. Understanding Smart Contracts

Smart contracts essentially trace their roots to blockchain, originally proffered as a core concept behind Ethereum's blockchain platform. A smart contract is a piece of software that extends blockchains far beyond their cryptocurrency function. They allow any kind of agreement, from rental contracts to securities, to be controlled and executed by software running on a blockchain. Once deployed onto a blockchain, they become entirely autonomous and self-executing - beyond the manipulation of any party, including their creators.

A real-world analogy can help to clarify their operation: consider a vending machine. When you insert a coin and select a product, the machine checks that enough payment has been made and then delivers the chosen product — automatically, without the need for human intervention. Smart contracts function similarly, but in a much more complex, programmable environment.

6.2. Benefits of Smart Contracts

Smart contracts bring forth a set of advantages that revolutionize the way transactions are conducted within the gig economy.

6.2.1. Trust

By eradicating the need for intermediaries, smart contracts build confidence among parties. Agreements are transparent and cannot be modified once set in motion, meaning no party can take advantage of another. This instills trust as professionals fully grasp the terms and conditions prior to committing, reassured that they can't be unexpectedly changed.

6.2.2. Accuracy and Transparency

Due to their programmable nature, smart contracts are precise and free from human error once deployed. Every stipulation within the contract is self-executing and leaves no room for misunderstanding. Additionally, the immutable nature of blockchain assures records and transactions can't be altered once sealed, promoting transparency.

6.2.3. Security

Powered by cutting-edge blockchain technology, smart contracts offer unparalleled security. Each contract is a line in the blockchain that is tamper-proof and immune to external hacks. This technology also prevents data loss as it is distributed across multiple nodes. These security features allow freelancers and clients to transact with confidence.

6.2.4. Speed and Efficiency

In the traditional model, paperwork is frequently a time-consuming endeavor. Smart contracts automate transactions, reducing the time and cost associated with manual processing and execution. Their self-executing nature also eliminates delays in settlements.

6.3. Smart Contracts and the Gig Economy

The gig economy, characterized by independent, decentralized workforces, strongly aligns with the attributes of blockchain and smart contracts. Blockchain-based platforms can facilitate swift and secure transactions between freelancers and their clients, ultimately empowering both parties.

6.3.1. Decentralized Marketplaces

Crypto-enabled decentralized marketplaces, facilitated by smart contracts, allow peer-to-peer transactions between service providers and consumers. Unlike current gig platforms often criticized for high fees and lack of transparency, these decentralized marketplaces offer a fair, transparent, and economically efficient alternative.

6.3.2. Secure and Timely Payments

Smart contracts can enforce stipulations where payments are automatically released upon completion of work terms, ensuring that freelancers receive their due compensation without delay or dispute. This workflow can advantageously replace traditional escrow services that often impose significant fees and potential Time delays.

6.3.3. Intellectual Property Protection

Smart contracts, combined with blockchain timestamping, can be utilized for copyright protection. Freelancers can upload an original design or content onto a blockchain, creating an immutable and time-stamped record reflecting their ownership.

6.4. Challenges and the Future

While smart contracts pose significant advancements in transaction facilitation within the gig economy, they aren't without challenges. Adoption requires digital literacy and some understanding of blockchain. Legal frameworks that recognize these contracts are still under development. Moreover, while blockchains themselves are highly secure, smart contracts are still software and are prone to bugs and vulnerabilities.

Despite these hurdles, the potential of smart contracts is significant. They are already transforming the digital gig economy and have the potential to affect far more. By delivering speed, security, and cost-efficiency, they can redefine the gig economy while empowering individual freelancers and entrepreneurs.

Embrace the exploration of this new frontier to unearth its potential.

Chapter 7. The Future of Payments: Cryptocurrencies and the Evolving Gig Economy

We live in a time of rapid digital evolution, where new technologies impact every aspect of our daily lives. Within the scope of our primary focus, the gig economy, one concept certainly stands out - the cryptocurrencies. As digital currencies that utilize cryptography for security, cryptocurrencies are catalyzing an unheralded transformation in the payment systems within the gig economy.

7.1. The Emergence of Cryptocurrencies

In 2008, amid the financial chaos, a still anonymous entity by the pseudonym 'Satoshi Nakamoto' introduced the concept of Bitcoin, a decentralized digital currency. This birthed the world's first cryptocurrency, and thus begun a new wave of digital finance. In Bitcoin's underlying technology, blockchain, Nakamoto not only solved the "double spend" issue but also provided the world with a clear way to verify transactions without needing a central authority.

As the years rolled by, numerous other cryptocurrencies have sprouted, including Ethereum, Ripple, and Litecoin. Today, over 5,000 unique cryptocurrencies exist, based on various blockchain technologies, each aiming at different niches and distinct uses within the digital economy.

7.2. Cryptocurrencies and The Gig Economy

The gig economy, characterized by short-term contracts or freelance work, has been growing exponentially, driven by the digitalization of our economy. Gig workers typically value flexibility and autonomy, often trading off traditional employment security. In such a dynamic environment, cryptocurrencies can provide several key advantages.

Firstly, cryptocurrencies offer reduced transaction costs. Traditional payment methods, such as bank transfers or payment gateways like Paypal, typically involve significant fees or commissions, which can eat up a substantial part of the gig worker's earnings. Cryptocurrencies, however, being decentralized, allow peer-to-peer transactions without an intermediary, thereby reducing these costs considerably.

Secondly, virtual currencies enable faster payments. With traditional banking systems, an international transfer may take several days to process. In contrast, cryptocurrency transactions can be completed in minutes, a vital feature for gig economy workers who often rely on prompt payments.

Lastly, cryptocurrencies can provide more significant financial inclusivity. For gig workers in developing countries or those without access to conventional banking services, being paid in cryptocurrencies can give them access to global markets that would otherwise be out of reach.

7.3. The Challenges Ahead

However, wide adoption of cryptocurrencies also poses challenges. The most prominent amongst them being its price volatility. Cryptocurrency prices can be extremely fluctuant, which can be a hurdle in an economy that requires stability in currency value for smooth functioning.

Regulation is another significant obstacle. Presently, different countries have disparate regulations for cryptocurrencies, ranging from full acceptance to outright ban. The lack of a standardized global framework for cryptocurrencies adds uncertainties to their use.

Lastly, lack of awareness and understanding of this technology is a barrier to adoption. Cryptocurrencies function based on complex technologies like cryptography and blockchain in which many people have little knowledge or understanding.

7.4. The Road Ahead

While cryptocurrencies are not fully poised to take over traditional payment systems just yet, they are making their presence felt. As blockchain technology evolves, solutions to the challenges are being pursued. Stablecoins, cryptocurrencies designed to minimize price volatility, are being introduced, and global bodies like the IMF are calling for international cooperation on regulating cryptocurrencies.

Moreover, crypto literacy is gradually improving, with an increasing number of people understanding the benefits and risks associated with them. Education in digital currencies is becoming a part of formal systems, with platforms offering courses on the same.

Prospective integration of cryptocurrencies into the gig economy's core payment structure could be a historical revolution that we are beginning to perceive. This revolution could further empower gig workers, making them truly independent, and facilitate their operations on a global platform.

The future of payments within the gig economy isn't set in stone. Much like the rest of the digital world we live in, it is subject to constant evolution and change. While there is significant work to be done and many battles to be fought, cryptocurrencies might well be a significant part of the gig economy's future, shaping the way brands and individuals interact and transact on a global scale. This transformation has the potential to take the gig economy to unprecedented heights, offering more freedom, control, and entrepreneurship opportunities to millions around the globe.

With unquestioned potential, the intertwining of cryptocurrency in the fabrics of gig economy is a development worth watching. As we step into the future seemingly filled with uncertainty, one thing remains absolute - change is an only constant, and as societies, we must learn to adapt and evolve.

Chapter 8. Blockchain's Role in Dispute Resolution for Freelancers

Blockchain technology has the potential to reframe the paradigms through which the gig economy operates. An area where blockchain particularly shines is in resolving disputes for freelancers. Its characteristics — decentralization, record immutability, smart contract automation, and others — can be instrumental in fostering fairer, more transparent, and quicker dispute resolution processes.

8.1. The Traditional Framework and Its Shortcomings

In the conventional gig economy infrastructure, dispute resolution is often characteristically slow and inefficient. Typically, a third-party intermediary is involved, usually an organization or platform that connects freelancers with clients. This entity oversees any disputes and makes a final decision. This setting can sometimes lead to bias, high costs, lack of transparency, and drawn-out resolution times.

Bias generally stems from these intermediaries generally leaning towards the clients who regularly use their platform and facilitate higher revenues. This system is often opaque, with neither parties privy to the entire dispute resolution process. High costs come into the equation in the form of fees that platforms charge freelancers and clients in the name of dispute mitigation. Further, these cases can take weeks or even months to resolve, causing significant time lags that can discourage freelancers and clients alike.

8.2. Blockchain as a Dispute Resolution Facilitator

Blockchain technology can alleviate many of these issues and streamline the dispute resolution process. Its decentralized nature brings equality to both parties involved in the dispute, removing the possibility of biased decisions.

Through smart contracts deployed on the blockchain, the terms of a project can be precisely defined and automatically enforced. These smart contracts trigger contingent upon certain predefined conditions being met. If a dispute arises, the immutable log of activity maintained by blockchain serves as a reliable reference point, ensuring that neither party can alter or dispute the facts.

Privacy remains protected as only the parties involved in the agreement, along with necessary entities like arbitrators, can access the contract details, assuring confidentiality. Blockchain eliminates the need for a centralized intermediary — reducing costs and expediting the resolution process — as the technology itself ensures enforcement and serves as the trust layer.

8.3. Smart Contracts and Beyond

Smart contracts are not self-sufficient dispute resolution mechanisms; however, they form a pivotal aspect of the process. These code-based contracts, predetermined and agreed upon by both parties, detail the terms of an agreement and their execution occurs automatically when certain conditions are met.

If a dispute arises, the smart contract halts, and the dispute resolution process begins. Due to the systems' decentralized nature, the arbitrating party should be elected or agreed upon. Once decided, the unalterable record of transactions and actions performed during the contract's tenure aids the arbitrator in making a fair judgment based on the data and conduct of both parties.

Once the decision is made, it's enforced, resulting in a quicker resolution, with transparency and non-bias comparatively higher than traditional systems.

8.4. Real-World Application, DAOs and Prediction Markets

A practical application of blockchain technology in facilitating disputes is Decentralized Autonomous Organizations (DAOs). DAOs can be tailored for freelancers and clients, enabling them to work under an autonomous, self-regulating system. DAOs use smart contracts to ensure predetermined rules, and in case of disputes, a peer-to-peer voting mechanism can resolve issues.

Another innovative application is Prediction markets. These are speculative markets created for making predictions, where the market prices can indicate what the crowd thinks the probability of the event is. This assessment can serve as an impartial resolution method, utilizing the wisdom of the crowd phenomenon.

8.5. Future Possibilities

Advancements in blockchain, like Layer 2 solutions and interoperability, promise to tackle current scalability issues, making blockchain adoption and use in dispute resolution viable. Integrating Artificial Intelligence (AI) could serve to further streamline the process by automatically evaluating the smart contract conduct and making preliminary decisions.

Blockchain promises to restructure the gig economy's existing dispute resolution infrastructure. Through decentralization, transparency, and automation, freelancers can look forward to a more equitable playground — free from bias, high costs, and prolonged waiting periods that currently plague the industry. However, it's essential to consider that concrete legal frameworks are needed to outline the functionality and legality of these systems legitimately. Only then can blockchain's full potential in dispute resolution be accurately harnessed.

Chapter 9. Case Studies: Blockchain Empowering Freelancers and Entrepreneurs

With an ethos grounded in transparency, trust, and security, blockchain technology is providing new pathways for freelancers and entrepreneurs. One of the channels through which this transformation is evident in the ascendant gig economy. Via a series of compelling case studies, we will journey into the heart of these changes, examining how individual professionals and startups are capitalizing on this technological zeitgeist.

9.1. Case Study 1: Freelance Graphic Designers and Blockchain

Blockchain's immutable and transparent nature renders it an ideal setting for freelance graphic designers. Consider the case of Jane, a graphic designer based in London. She was frequently troubled by delayed payments, lack of contract enforcement, and occasional copyright infringements. With blockchain, she found a solution.

Jane started using a blockchain-based freelancing platform for her projects. The platform incorporated smart contracts—self-executing contracts where terms and protocols are directly written into code, then stored and replicated on the blockchain, excluding the need for a middleman. This meant her terms of agreement with clients were automatically enforced.

Additionally, the payment mechanism was tied to the completion of predetermined milestones, guaranteeing timely payment. Handling her network's interactions on a decentralized peer-to-peer network afforded Jane autonomy and control over her transactions.

By leveraging these elements, Jane addressed her initial challenges. Efficient copyright management, contract enforcement, and prompt payments became her new norm. Here, blockchain empowered a solo graphic designer to redefine her work system, significantly boosting her professional experience.

9.2. Case Study 2: Small-Scale Food Producers and Blockchain

For small-scale food producers, blockchain can aid in supply chain transparency and trust. Consider a group of organic farmers in Vietnam, grappling with trust issues from consumers dubious about their organically grown claim.

To establish trust, the farmers adopted blockchain-based traceability solutions. Each produce's journey, from farm to fork, was recorded on the blockchain—growing conditions, harvesting, processing, packing, and finally, selling. Consumers could view this information by scanning a QR code attached to the produce.

As a result, public trust in their product soared. Thanks to the transparency, consumers were convinced of the product's authenticity, which resulted in increased sales.

9.3. Case Study 3: Small Tech Startups and Blockchain

In our third case, we illustrate how blockchain helps small tech startups compete with larger corporations. A tiny game development enterprise in Estonia, crushed under the monopolies of game distribution giants, used blockchain to turn the tables.

The firm released their game on a blockchain-based distribution platform. This platform, decentralized and operating on smart contract protocols, removed the need for a middleman. Consequently, the lion's share of profits from game sales went directly to the game developers.

Moreover, transactions were executed in cryptocurrencies, reducing costs and time involved in currency conversions for international sales. The blockchain platform also provided more transparency about sales data, enabling the small company to compete effectively in the market.

9.4. Case Study 4: Blockchain and the Gig Economy

A gig-based online platform based in the US, facing difficulties in international transactions due to exchange rates and banking fees, utilized blockchain to streamline their operation.

The platform started operating on a blockchain-based ecosystem, accepting cryptocurrencies for services rendered. The introduction of smart contracts ensured seamless execution of agreements. With tokens pegged to a stable fiat currency, they eradicated exchange fluctuation issues.

The platform's transition to blockchain turned it into a more accessible, equitable, and cost-effective operation. The reduced transactional friction made it a more attractive proposition for global freelancers and employers alike, driving the gig economy forward.

In conclusion, from individual freelancers to small-scale producers and entrepreneurs, blockchain presents ground-breaking opportunities for solving problems and fostering trust, transparency, and security. It is evident from these case studies that this powerful technology breeds innovation and nurtures an environment that enables anyone engaging in the gig economy to thrive. Blockchain's empowerment of the gig economy heralds a new dawn in employment—one where autonomy, control, and entrepreneurship prevail.

Chapter 10. Challenges and Risks: Navigating Through the Blockchain-Powered Gig Economy

Before we delve into the exhilarating possibilities that the blockchain enabled gig economy envisages, it is essential to acknowledge and understand the challenges and risks tied to this burgeoning frontier. This multi-faceted section will guide you through practical ways to navigate these challenges and make the most of the blockchain's profound transformative power in this realm.

10.1. Understanding New technology

Notwithstanding its potential, blockchain remains a novelty and understanding its workings can be convoluted. It is built on complex mathematical and cryptographic principles. While mastering these principles isn't essential for participants in the gig economy, a baseline understanding of how blockchain works and its core features is crucial.

The basic structure is that of a decentralized ledger system where transactions are recorded in multiple locations (nodes) concurrently. Although this provides overarching benefits like enhanced security, the decryption and proof-of-work processes can be perplexing to beginners. Use resources like online tutorials, webinars, and community forums to familiarize yourself with the basics and gradually increase your understanding.

The adoption rate can be potentially slowed down by this learning curve, however, as technology advances and systems become more user-friendly, this barrier will diminish.

10.2. Regulatory Uncertainity

Blockchain technology posits unique challenges to regulatory frameworks around the world. Laws and regulations pertaining to data privacy, monetary transactions, and digital assets are yet to fully adapt to blockchain's novel nature, leading to uncertain legal landscapes.

One notable area of ambiguity is taxation. As gig economy professionals may likely earn in cryptocurrencies enabled by the blockchain, how these earnings are to be reported and taxed remains unclear. This gap leaves participants open to inadvertent non-compliance.

A forward-looking approach for freelancers and entrepreneurs is to actively follow regulatory developments in this field, consult with legal experts, and form associations to collectively advocate for fair and clear regulation.

10.3. Volatility of Cryptocurrency

A key element of most blockchain ecosystems is the use of cryptocurrencies for transactions. While this offers freedom from traditional banking constraints, it adds an element of volatility and risk to gig economy earnings.

Cryptocurrency prices can fluctuate markedly due to market dynamics, causing instability of value. This price instability may deter freelancers who value stable income. To manage this risk, consider using strategies like hedging and diversifying your cryptocurrency portfolio.

Additionally, some blockchain platforms are developing stablecoins—cryptocurrencies pegged to stable assets—to mitigate this risk.

10.4. Cybersecurity

Despite the enhanced security offered by the blockchain's structural features, it's crucial not to overlook the potential for cybersecurity threats. The irreversible nature of blockchain transactions, combined with the potential anonymity of bad actors, can make theft or fraud challenging to manage.

For digital wallets used in storing transactional cryptocurrencies, employ robust security measures like hardware wallets or encrypted wallets. Be cautious with sharing details online and be updated on potential scam threats.

10.5. Contractual Disputeness

Smart contracts automate transactions based on predefined conditions. While this can bring about increased efficiency, disputes can arise from incorrect or ambiguous definitions within those contracts. Remember that smart contracts are as effective as their programming; human errors in their coding can lead to unintended outcomes.

To mitigate contract disputes, invest in well-drafted contract templates and engage professionals if required. Additionally, consider using dispute resolution services offered by certain blockchain platforms.

10.6. Environmental Impact

The energy consumption associated with blockchain, specifically proof-of-work (where extensive computational energy is used to validate transactions), has raised environmental concerns. As we combat climate change, the energy-efficient alternatives must be prioritized.

Exploring proof-of-stake and other consensus methods should be a consistent practice for gig economy participants interested in making responsible environmental decisions.

Nevertheless, it's imperative to keep in mind that these challenges are not insurmountable. The warp-speed technological advancements, increasing adoption, evolving regulatory landscapes, and rising awareness are all inching towards reducing these barriers. Brace yourself to traverse through this changing landscape, as not only can these risks be managed with awareness and caution but they can provide an opportunity for blockchain to flourish into the transformative force it embodies.

Chapter 11. Embracing the Future: Strategies for Thriving in a Blockchain-Driven Gig Economy

The future of the gig economy is pivoted on the adaptation and scaling of innovative technology. Instinctively, one might think of the ubiquity of smartphones and apps that have facilitated the rise of the gig economy. Still, another technological breakthrough—blockchain—is set to drive the sector into its next stage of evolution.

Blockchain technology, born out of the development of Bitcoin, is a transparent, encrypted, and decentralized database. Attributes that make it a perfect solution to solve some of the most significant challenges the freelance and entrepreneurial sectors currently face.

11.1. Grasping the Concept of Blockchain

In its simplest form, a blockchain is a type of database. It's a way of storing information that heightens transparency, security, and decentralization. The name essentially gives its function away - a chain of blocks. Here, blocks refer to digital information and chain refers to the public database.

The blocks store information about who is participating in transactions, when transactions occur, and distinguishable elements about the trades themselves. Once a block is filled with data, it is added to the chain, thus forming a blockchain.

Blockchain technology offers a more autonomous and democratic platform for transactions, effectively removing the need for intermediaries. As it continuously self-audits every transaction, manipulations become virtually impossible, lending an unwavering sense of trust and security, key qualities sought after in the gig economy.

11.2. Embracing Blockchain for a Thriving Gig Economy

The gig economy has existed in one form or another for centuries, but advancements in technology have allowed this economic model to evolve and expand. However, this evolution isn't without its issues, and participants in the gig economy have long suffered the consequences of a lack of transparent payment structures, security, and trust.

That's where blockchain comes in. The highly secure system of blockchain can be utilized in the gig economy for smart contracts, assurance of payment, and to reduce the need for middlemen.

Let's delve further into how these work.

11.2.1. Smart Contracts

Inherently included in blockchain, Cmart Contracts are self-executing contracts with the terms of the agreement between buyer and seller directly written into the code. The code is controlled by the blockchain network, thus eliminating the need for a third party, ensuring more transparency and less chances of breaches.

11.2.2. Assurance of Payment

One of the major setbacks for freelancers currently is the lack of guarantee for payment. Blockchain eradicates this issue via its transparency and traceability. Payment gets locked into device and only released upon task completion, this eradicates the risk of non-payment scenarios and contributes to a more flexible and fair gig economy.

11.2.3. Reducing Need for Intermediaries

While platforms like Fiverr or Upwork have their positives, they also take a substantial cut from freelancers' earnings as 'service charges'. Blockchain helps eliminate this scenario by allowing direct transactions between clients and freelancers.

11.3. Strategies for Thriving in a Blockchain-Driven Gig Economy

Once we understand the immense potential of integrating blockchain into a gig economy, it becomes essential to strategize ways to thrive in this evolving landscape.

11.3.1. Educate Yourself

The first step to thriving in a blockchain-run gig economy is to fully understand how blockchain works. It's vital to understand how smart contracts work, what it means for a system to be decentralized, and how transactions get validated within the blockchain system.

11.3.2. Update Your Skills

As with any significant technological shift, there will be a need for new skills. Blockchain will be no different. Ensure that you have the skills, not just to use blockchain applications, but to understand, troubleshoot, and even innovate upon these solutions.

11.3.3. Learn the Laws

Legal and regulatory aspects of blockchain are still unclear and can vary greatly between jurisdictions. To protect yourself and your business, it's important that you understand current laws surrounding blockchain technologies and follow updates closely.

11.3.4. Build the Right Network

Networking remains crucial in a blockchain-powered gig economy. Engage yourself with blockchain communities to keep up with trends, make contact with other professionals in the field, and continue your learning process through shared knowledge.

Blockchain has the potential to revolutionise the gig economy by solving long-standing issues of trust, security, and transparency, empowering both service providers and service seekers. While the shift needs a strategic understanding and approach, it merely spells the dawn of a new and aspiring era in the lifestyle of freelance work and entrepreneurship. An era of transparency, trust, security, independence, flexibility, and unprecedented growth.

In the end, the key lies in embracing the change rather than resisting it, and those who accustom themselves to the rhythm of this progression are bound to taste success in the near future.